HIGHER

2006

[BLANK PAGE]

OFFICIAL SQA PAST PAPERS WITH ANSWERS

HIGHER

GERMAN
2006-2009

First exam published in 2006.

Published by Bright Red Publishing Ltd, 6 Stafford Street, Edinburgh EH3 7AU

tel: 0131 220 5804 fax: 0131 220 6710 info@brightredpublishing.co.uk www.brightredpublishing.co.uk

ISBN 978-1-84948-060-4

A CIP Catalogue record for this book is available from the British Library.

Bright Red Publishing is grateful to the copyright holders, as credited on the final page of the book, for permission to use their material.

Every effort has been made to trace the copyright holders and to obtain their permission for the use of copyright material.

Bright Red Publishing will be happy to receive information allowing us to rectify any error or omission in future editions.

X060/301

NATIONAL QUALIFICATIONS 2006	WEDNESDAY, 24 MAY 9.00 AM – 10.40 AM	**GERMAN** HIGHER Reading and Directed Writing

45 marks are allocated to this paper. The value attached to each question is shown after each question.

You should spend approximately one hour on Section I and 40 minutes on Section II.

You may use a German dictionary.

SCOTTISH QUALIFICATIONS AUTHORITY

SECTION I—READING

Read this magazine article carefully then answer **in English** the questions which follow it.
This article deals with school students in Hersbruck (Bavaria) who have part-time jobs.

Für Handy, Klamotten, Kino, Urlaub

Schüler bessern sich durch Jobs ihr Taschengeld auf—Die Schulleistung darf nicht darunter leiden.

Handy, Klamotten, Kino und Urlaub—das Leben eines Schülers kann ganz schön teuer werden. Dafür reicht das Taschengeld meist nicht aus, das wissen viele Jugendliche aus
5 leidvoller Erfahrung. Ferienjobs sind für sie deshalb eine willkommene Alternative zum elterlichen Geldbeutel. Mittlerweile gibt es aber zahlreiche Schüler, die nicht nur in den Ferien, sondern regelmäßig neben der
10 Schule arbeiten, um ihr eigenes Geld zu verdienen.

Einer von ihnen ist Sebastian Herbst. Zweimal pro Woche schwingt er sich in den Fahrradsattel, um Fernsehzeitschriften und
15 Illustrierte auszutragen. Seit zwei Jahren verschafft sich der 17-Jährige, der in die zehnte Klasse des Paul-Pfinzing-Gymnasiums geht, damit ein Stück finanzieller Unabhängigkeit von seinen
20 Eltern.

Das verdiente Geld gibt er hauptsächlich für Handy und Klamotten aus. Auch den Schüleraustausch nach Frankreich und die diesjährige Reise nach Schottland will er
25 damit bezahlen. Dass er den Job überhaupt bekommen hat, hat Sebastian eigentlich seiner Mutter zu verdanken, die damals in der Zeitung die Stellenanzeige las.

Die Arbeit selbst ist für ihn mittlerweile
30 zur reinen Routine geworden. So hat er sich den Bezirk, für den er zuständig ist, in drei Touren eingeteilt, die er dann nacheinander mit dem Fahrrad abfährt. Bei jedem Wetter natürlich, denn die Kunden wollen ihre
35 abonnierten Zeitschriften ja auch rechtzeitig erhalten. „Man muss sich an die Zeiten und Termine halten", sagt Sebastian. „Aber wenn es heiß ist oder wenn Glatteis ist, ist es schon blöd", gesteht er lächelnd: „Der Job
40 macht mir viel Spaß; es ist immerhin leicht verdientes Geld und meine Schularbeit leidet ja auch nicht darunter."

Finanzielle Unabhängigkeit war auch das Ziel von Susanne Hupfer. Früher jobbte sie gelegentlich als Babysitterin, seit längerem 45 bedient die 17-jährige Realschülerin nun aber schon im Café Corretto. Im Laden sah sie vor zwei Jahren das Stellengesuch aushängen, bewarb sich und nach einem Probearbeitstag hatte sie den Job. „Ein 50 Grund, warum ich unbedingt kellnern wollte, ist, weil zu dem Stundenlohn auch noch das Trinkgeld dazukommt", erklärt sie. „Zudem ist die Arbeit äußerst abwechslungsreich, denn jeder Gast ist 55 schließlich anders. Der Umgang mit den Menschen fällt mir aber leicht. Man lernt schnell, locker auf die Leute zuzugehen und auch unfreundlichen Gästen gegenüber freundlich zu sein. Aber es gibt Tage, da ist 60 es schon stressig."

Wegen der Abschlussprüfungen an der Realschule musste Susanne weniger Stunden machen, damit die Arbeit als Kellnerin ihre Schulnoten nicht beeinträchtigt. In der Tat 65 findet sie das Gegenteil: „In Kopfrechnen bin ich echt besser geworden", sagt sie lachend.

Auch Andreas Förthner arbeitet seit über zwei Jahren in direktem Kundenkontakt. In 70 einem Supermarkt räumt er zweimal pro Woche die Regale ein oder ist in der Getränkeabteilung für [1]das Leergut zuständig. Seine Eltern finden es schon gut, dass sich der 18-jährige Gymnasiast sein 75 eigenes Geld verdient. „Sein Bruder hat diesen Job früher immerhin auch einmal gemacht und mit der Schule hat es bislang auch keine Probleme gegeben", sagen sie.

„Ich weiß genau, wo man alles im 80 Supermarkt finden kann und welche Flaschen wir zurücknehmen dürfen", sagt Andreas. Wenn Kunden genervt und unfreundlich sind, hat er seine eigene Taktik entwickelt: „Man muss sympathisch sein und 85 den Kunden helfen."

Die Arbeit macht ihm Spaß und er verdient ja gut damit, aber vor allem ist sich Andreas über eines im Klaren: „Es ist eine gute
90 Erfahrung. Man bekommt ein anderes Gefühl fürs Geld und überlegt sich, wofür man es ausgibt; aber lebenslang möchte ich das auch nicht machen."

[1]**das Leergut = the empties**

QUESTIONS

Marks

1. Why do many young people find that they need a part-time job?

2 points

2. Sebastian Herbst is one of these students.

   (*a*) What exactly does he do?

   1 point

   (*b*) What **two** major expenses does he want to pay for?

   1 point

   (*c*) How did he come by his job?

   1 point

3. Read lines 29–42.

   (*a*) How does Sebastian organise his work?

   2 points

   (*b*) What comment does he make about the weather?

   1 point

   (*c*) What **two** things does Sebastian say about his job?

   1 point

Now read lines 43–61.

4. (*a*) What motivated Susanne Hupfer to find work?

   1 point

   (*b*) Why did she particularly want to be a waitress?

   1 point

5. What does Susanne say about dealing with people?

   2 points

6. Read lines 62–68.

   (*a*) Why is Susanne working fewer hours just now?

   1 point

   (*b*) In what way has her job helped her at school?

   1 point

7. Read lines 69–79.

   (*a*) What does Andreas' job involve?

   2 points

   (*b*) Why do his parents have no objections to his working?

   2 points

8. Read lines 87–93.

   Why does Andreas feel his job has been a good experience?

   1 point

9. Translate into English:

   „Ich weiß genau, . . . den Kunden helfen." (lines 80–86)

   (20 points)

   = 20 marks

   10

   (30)

[Turn over for SECTION II on *Page four*

SECTION II—DIRECTED WRITING

Marks

You recently took part in an exchange visit to Germany. One day your host family took you on a trip to a town some distance away.

On your return to Scotland, you send in an article **in German** for the newspaper of your exchange partner's school.

You must include the following information and **you should try to add** other relevant details:

- who all were in your host family and what their home was like

- what the family's local area was like and what there was to do there

- how the family spent a typical day

- what you did on the day you went on this special trip

- what you all did for food that day

- whether you would recommend the experience of an exchange trip to someone else.

Your report should be 150 – 180 words in length.

Marks will be deducted for any area of information that is omitted.   **(15)**

[END OF QUESTION PAPER]

X060/303

NATIONAL QUALIFICATIONS 2006	WEDNESDAY, 24 MAY 11.00 AM – 12.00 NOON	**GERMAN HIGHER** Listening Transcript

This paper must not be seen by any candidate.

The material overleaf is provided for use in an emergency only (eg the recording or equipment proving faulty) or where permission has been given in advance by SQA for the material to be read to candidates with additional support needs. The material must be read exactly as printed.

SCOTTISH QUALIFICATIONS AUTHORITY

©

Instructions to reader(s):

The dialogue below should be read in approximately 3 minutes. On completion of the first reading, pause for two minutes, then read the dialogue a second time.

Where special arrangements have been agreed in advance to allow the reading of the material, those sections marked **(m)** should be read by a male speaker and those marked **(f)** by a female.

Katherina, a 21 year-old German who is studying in Scotland, talks about issues concerning a healthy lifestyle.

(m) **Ist für dich die Gesundheit wichtig?**

(f) Ja, die Gesundheit ist für mich sehr wichtig. Ich denke, dass Jugendliche fit sein sollten, damit sie auch noch gesund bleiben, wenn sie älter sind.

(m) **Was machst du denn, um fit zu bleiben?**

(f) Ich gehe regelmäßig mit meiner Freundin zusammen joggen, nehme am Badminton-Unterricht teil und spiele zweimal die Woche Volleyball.

(m) **Und passt du auf, was du isst ?**

(f) Ja, ich denke schon. Ich würde jetzt nicht jeden Tag zu McDonalds gehen oder mich von Fastfood ernähren, sondern achte schon darauf, dass ich viel Salat und Gemüse esse.

(m) **Ist Fastfood denn bei euch in Deutschland genauso beliebt wie hier in Schottland?**

(f) Ich denke, in Deutschland gehen weniger Leute zu McDonalds oder Burger King, aber hier in Schottland habe ich festgestellt, dass ganz viele Familien mit jungen Kindern sich von Fastfood ernähren.

(m) **Und apropos gesundes Essen, haben deine Eltern in dieser Sache immer ein gutes Beispiel gegeben?**

(f) Meine Eltern haben immer sehr darauf geachtet, dass wir jeden Tag viel Obst und nicht zu viel Süßigkeiten gegessen haben.

(m) **Und wie oft trinkst du Alkohol?**

(f) Ich trinke manchmal am Wochenende. Ab und zu ein Bier, aber nicht sehr regelmäßig.

(m) **Und gibt es ein Alkoholproblem in Deutschland?**

(f) In den Großstädten gibt es sicherlich ein Problem mit Alkohol. Aber ich denke, nicht mehr oder weniger als hier in Schottland. Ich glaube, das ist ziemlich gleich.

In Deutschland können die Jugendlichen schon mit 16 Bier oder Wein trinken und diese Getränke auch legal im Laden oder in einer Kneipe kaufen.

(m) **Wie steht's denn mit dem Rauchen? Das passt doch nicht zu einem gesunden Leben, oder?**

(f) Nein, Rauchen ist natürlich sehr ungesund. Ich selber rauche nicht und habe nie geraucht. Viele Jugendliche rauchen aber, weil es cool ist; Gruppenzwang—dann raucht man eben zusammen mal eine Zigarette. Ich denke, das ist in allen Ländern gleich.

(m) **Gibt es Unterschiede zwischen Schottland und Deutschland bezüglich der Gesundheit?**

(f) Ja, es gibt große Unterschiede. Es ist mir aufgefallen, dass sehr viele Menschen in Schottland zu dick sind und Gesundheitsprobleme haben, auf Grund ihres Gewichts. Hier sehe ich auch kleine Kinder, die sehr dick sind und keinen Sport treiben können. In Deutschland ist das nicht der Fall, meiner Meinung nach.

(m) **Woran liegt das?**

(f) In deutschen Schulen essen die meisten Kinder in der Pause ein Butterbrot oder einen Apfel, und man darf in der Schule keine Süßigkeiten verkaufen. Hier in Schottland sehe ich in den Pausen ganz viele Kinder mit Chipstüten herumstehen. So was kommt in Deutschland nicht vor. Und fast jedes Kind treibt auch am Nachmittag Sport, denn bei uns gibt es viele Sportvereine für Jugendliche.

[END OF TRANSCRIPT]

[BLANK PAGE]

FOR OFFICIAL USE

Examiner's Marks	
A	
B	

Total
Mark

X060/302

NATIONAL
QUALIFICATIONS
2006

WEDNESDAY, 24 MAY
11.00 AM – 12.00 NOON

GERMAN
HIGHER
Listening/Writing

Fill in these boxes and read what is printed below.

Full name of centre

Town

Forename(s)

Surname

Date of birth

Day   Month   Year   Scottish candidate number   Number of seat

Do not open this paper until told to do so.

Answer Section A **in English** and Section B **in German**.

Section A

Listen carefully to the recording with a view to answering, **in English**, the questions printed in this answer book. Write your answers **clearly** and **legibly** in the spaces provided after each question.

You will have 2 minutes to study the questions before hearing the recording.

The recording will be played **twice**, with an interval of 2 minutes between the two playings.

You may make notes at any time but only in this answer book. **Draw your pen through any notes before you hand in the book.**

Move on to Section B when you have completed Section A: you will **not** be told when to do this.

Section B

Do not write your response in this book: **use the 4 page lined answer sheet**.

You will be told to insert the answer sheet inside this book before handing in your work.

You may consult a German dictionary at any time during **both** sections.

Before leaving the examination room you must give this book to the invigilator. If you do not, you may lose all the marks for this paper.

SCOTTISH
QUALIFICATIONS
AUTHORITY

Section A

Marks

Katherina, a 21 year-old German who is studying in Scotland, talks about issues concerning a healthy lifestyle.

1. Why does Katherina think that young people should keep fit?

1 point

2. What does Katherina do to keep fit?

2 points

3. In what ways does Katherina watch what she eats?

2 points

4. What differences concerning fast food does Katherina notice between Germany and Scotland?

2 points

5. How did Katherina's parents make sure she ate healthily?

2 points

Marks

6. How often does she drink alcohol? **1 point**

7. (*a*) To what extent does Katherina think there is an alcohol problem in Germany? **1 point**

(*b*) What is the law in Germany with regard to alcohol and young people? **2 points**

8. What does Katherina say about smoking? **2 points**

9. What health issues has she noticed in Scotland? **2 points**

10. Why does Katherina think that children in Germany are not as overweight as many in Scotland? **3 points**

(20 points)

= 20 marks

[Turn over for Section B on *Page four*

Marks

Section B

Und du, ist für dich die Gesundheit wichtig? Passt du darauf auf, was du isst und trinkst? Was hältst du von Alkohol und Zigaretten?

Schreibe 120 – 150 Worte zu diesen Fragen!

10

(30)

USE THE 4 PAGE LINED ANSWER SHEET FOR YOUR ANSWER TO SECTION B

[END OF QUESTION PAPER]

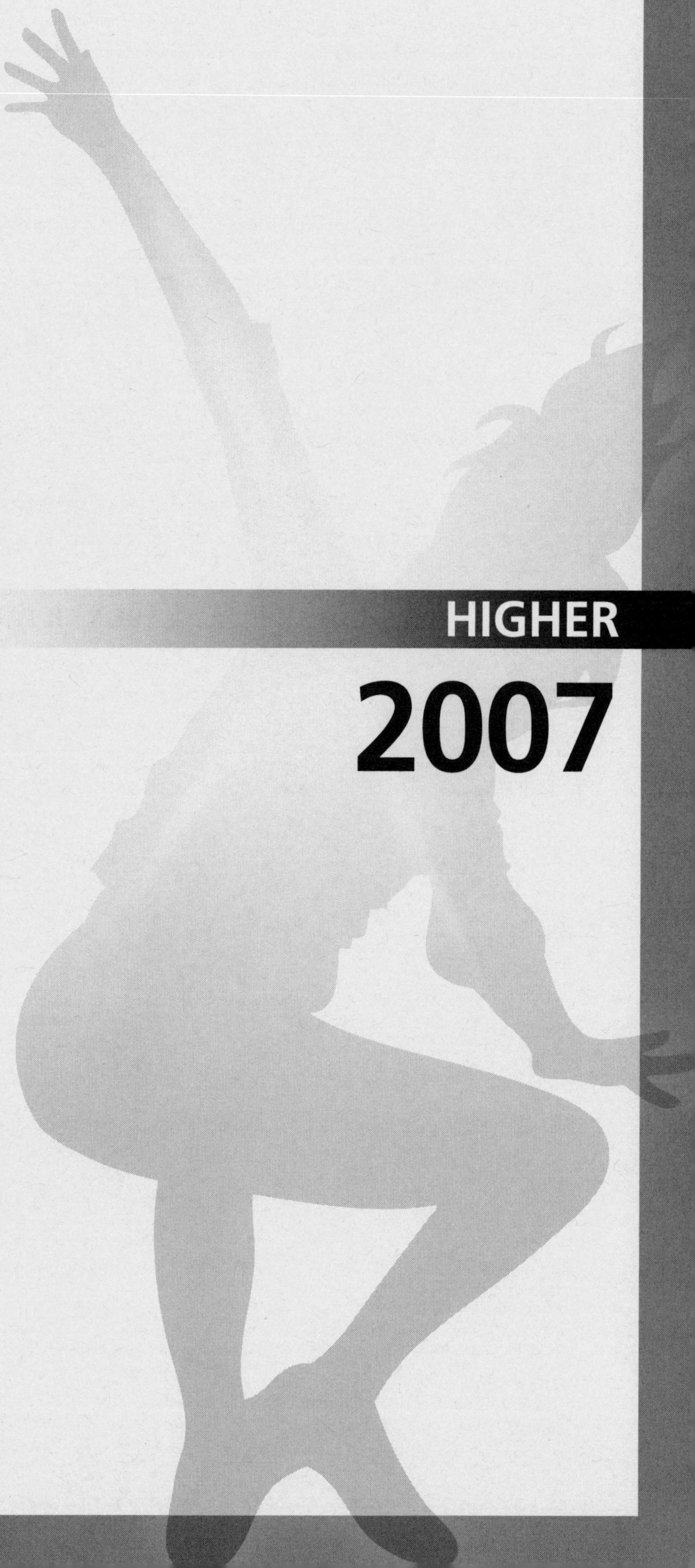

HIGHER

2007

[BLANK PAGE]

X060/301

NATIONAL QUALIFICATIONS 2007	WEDNESDAY, 30 MAY 9.00 AM – 10.40 AM	**GERMAN** HIGHER Reading and Directed Writing

45 marks are allocated to this paper. The value attached to each question is shown after each question.

You should spend approximately one hour on Section I and 40 minutes on Section II.

You may use a German dictionary.

SCOTTISH QUALIFICATIONS AUTHORITY

SECTION I—READING

Read this magazine article carefully then answer **in English** the questions which follow it.

This article is about Germans who are thinking about or are actually living in Australia.

Wie ist es wirklich, fern der Heimat zu leben?

Immer mehr Deutsche wollen nach Australien. Ulrich Blos, zum Beispiel, träumt seit sechs Jahren von Australien. „Ich habe hier in Deutschland eine gute
5 Arbeit", sagt er, aber seit er 2001 eine Weile auf einer australischen Farm gearbeitet hat, hat er diesen Traum. „Wir sind im Busch gewandert. Da war nur Wald, nur Natur, so weit das Auge reicht. Deutschland ist mir
10 jetzt zu eng. Es gibt zu viel Stress und Leistungsdruck. Ob und wann wir tatsächlich nach Australien gehen, weiß ich noch nicht. Vielleicht, wenn die Kinder erwachsen sind."

15 Marie Merkel ist Krankenschwester in *Berlin*. „Mit meinen Qualifikationen habe ich in Australien gute Chancen. Ich würde natürlich meine dreijährige Tochter mitnehmen. Mit vier Jahren könnte sie dort
20 in die Schule gehen." Eigentlich gibt es für sie nur eine Hürde: die hohen Kosten für die Visa und den beruflichen Qualifikations-Test. Insgesamt würde es wohl etwa 2000 australische Dollar kosten und so viel Geld
25 hat sie nicht.

Gerhard Scheller hat seinen deutschen Pass abgegeben und ist jetzt stolz darauf, australischer Staatsbürger zu sein. Gerhard und seine Frau Britta haben sich kennen
30 gelernt, als sie in *Hamburg* Informatik studierten. Seit 1994 leben sie in einem Vorort von *Sydney*. Zurückkehren wollen sie nicht: Er begann in Australien mit einem eigenen Betrieb, seit sieben Jahren fährt er
35 Trucks. Sein Fotoalbum erzählt eine Geschichte vom selbst ausgebauten Haus mit Garten, von schönen Tagen am Meer und Festen mit Freunden. „Der Anfang kann einsam sein, wenn man stumm in der Ecke
40 sitzt und nicht einmal Witze auf Englisch verstehen kann", sagt Gerhard. „Und um mit Australiern reden zu können, muss man etwas über Politik, Sport und Humor in Australien wissen."

45 „Und noch etwas sollten künftige Auswanderer bedenken", sagt Gerhard: „Es kostet sehr viel Geld und Zeit, wieder nach Deutschland zu kommen. Wir waren erst nach acht Jahren das erste Mal in der Lage, für vier Wochen nach Deutschland zu
50 fliegen." Gerhards Fotos erzählen auch von der harten Arbeit hinter dem australischen Traum. Oft arbeitet er sechs Tage die Woche. „Ich habe noch nie in meinem Leben so lange und so hart gearbeitet. Keine
55 Mittagspause trotz 40 Grad im Schatten—die Leute hier arbeiten einfach weiter. Der Lohn ist geringer als in Deutschland und die Lebenshaltungskosten in *Sydney* viel höher." Was vermisst er an
60 Deutschland? Gerhard lacht. „Currywurst. Die bekomme ich hier nirgendwo." Heimweh kann auch die Form einer Wurst annehmen.

Für Antje Eildermann ist Australien ein
65 Geruch und ein Lachen. „Es riecht hier oft wochenlang nach Rauch", sagt Antje, die vor zwei Jahren von *Berlin* nach *Sydney* gezogen ist. Der Rauch kommt ab August von den Waldbränden in den Blue Mountains. Das
70 Lachen stammt von einem Vogel. Es ist der Ruf des Kookaburra, eines australischen Vogels, der hier überall vorkommt. Eigentlich wollte Antje gar nicht auswandern, sondern kam nach dem
75 Studium zum Praktikum. „Dann habe ich Marcel getroffen, geheiratet und bin geblieben." Manchmal vermisst sie Deutschland—„nicht das Land, eher den Alltag, den [1]Tchibo um die Ecke oder so,
80 aber ich liebe *Sydney*. Die Menschen sind sehr offen, man knüpft schnell Kontakte."

„Das Schulsystem finde ich aber nicht so gut," sagt Antje. „Gute Schulen sind in Australien in der Regel privat und relativ
85 teuer." Noch haben die beiden keine Kinder, „aber wenn wir Kinder bekommen, sollten sie eher in Deutschland zu Schule gehen", sagt sie. Es gibt diesen Plan, nach *Berlin* zurückzuziehen. „Mein Mann würde
90 mitkommen, er liebt Deutschland und war schon oft da", sagt sie. Sie möchte auch aus

beruflichen Gründen zurückkehren. Ihre Eltern haben eine Firma in *Berlin*, die Antje 95 eines Tages übernehmen möchte. „In drei bis fünf Jahren," sagt Antje, „werden wir nach Deutschland auswandern." Vielleicht wird sie dann eines Tages, auf dem Weg zum

¹Tchibo, einen eingebildeten Feuergeruch wahrnehmen und ein Lachen vermissen. 100 Heimweh ist ein vielseitiges Gefühl.

¹Tchibo = a shop selling a brand of German coffee

QUESTIONS

Marks

1. (a) What experience made Ulrich Blos start dreaming about a life in Australia? **1 point**

   (b) How does he feel about Germany now? **2 points**

   (c) When might he go to Australia to live? **1 point**

2. Read lines 15–25.

   (a) Why is Marie Merkel thinking about moving to Australia? **2 points**

   (b) What is the only thing that is stopping her from going? **1 point**

3. Read lines 26–44.

   What does Gerhard Scheller say about starting a new life in Australia? **2 points**

4. Now read lines 45–64.

   (a) What do Germans thinking of emigrating to Australia need to be aware of, according to Gerhard? **1 point**

   (b) What information does Gerhard give about his working life? Mention **three** things. **3 points**

5. Read lines 65–82.

   (a) What sums up Australia as far as Antje Eildermann is concerned? **2 points**

   (b) Antje never intended to emigrate. Why did she stay in Australia? **1 point**

   (c) What does she like about people in Sydney? **1 point**

6. Read lines 83–101.

   (a) What does Antje say about schools in Australia? **1 point**

   (b) Why will they probably return to Berlin one day? **2 points**

   (20 points)

   = 20 marks

7. Translate into English:

   „Gerhard Scheller hat . . . Vorort von *Sydney*." (lines 26–32) **10**

   (30)

[Turn over for SECTION II on *Page four*

SECTION II—DIRECTED WRITING

Marks

You have travelled to Germany to spend a holiday with German friends of your parents. While you are there, you are asked to baby-sit one day from 3.00 pm until 8.00 pm.

When you return to Scotland, you have to write a report **in German** for the Languages department in your school/college.

You must include the following information and **you should try to add** other relevant details:

- what the journey to Germany was like and how you felt travelling on your own
- who all was in the family and what they were like
- where the family house was situated and what it was like
- how you spent the five hours with the children while their parents were out
- what you did usually on your other evenings while in Germany
- why you would/would not baby-sit for this German family again.

Your report should be 150 – 180 words in length.

Marks will be deducted for any area of information that is omitted.   **(15)**

[END OF QUESTION PAPER]

X060/303

NATIONAL QUALIFICATIONS 2007	WEDNESDAY, 30 MAY 11.00 AM – 12.00 NOON	GERMAN HIGHER Listening Transcript

This paper must not be seen by any candidate.

The material overleaf is provided for use in an emergency only (eg the recording or equipment proving faulty) or where permission has been given in advance by SQA for the material to be read to candidates with additional support needs. The material must be read exactly as printed.

SCOTTISH
QUALIFICATIONS
AUTHORITY

©

Instructions to reader(s):

The dialogue below should be read in approximately 4 minutes. On completion of the first reading, pause for two minutes, then read the dialogue a second time.

Where special arrangements have been agreed in advance to allow the reading of the material, those sections marked **(m)** should be read by a male speaker and those marked **(f)** by a female.

Candidates have two minutes to study the questions before the transcript is read.

Nicole, a German-language assistant, is interviewed about her Abitur and what she did after the exams.

(m)   Nicole, du hast letztes Jahr Abitur gemacht. Wie war diese Zeit für dich?

(f)   Ja, ich habe letzten Mai Abitur gemacht. Das war eine sehr stressige Zeit. Wir hatten wahnsinnig viel zu tun. Es gab viel zu lernen, viele Bücher zu lesen und Aufsätze zu schreiben. Ich hatte damals sehr viel Stress; ich erinnere mich noch ganz gut an alles.

(m)   Wie hast du dich darauf vorbereitet—also auf das Abitur?

(f)   Wir haben einen Lernplan gemacht, um den ganzen Stoff unterzubringen. Wir haben von Woche zu Woche verschiedene Sachen gelernt und das immer wiederholt. Ich hatte überhaupt keine Freizeit mehr. Ich konnte meine Freunde nicht mehr so oft treffen und hatte fast keine Zeit mehr, Sport zu machen. Und ja, die Zeit war einfach sehr knapp.

(m)   Und wie ist das Abitur gelaufen?

(f)   Es ist gut gelaufen. Ich war sehr zufrieden mit meinen Noten; ich hatte einen Durchschnitt von 1,5, was sehr gut ist.

(m)   Was habt ihr nach dem vielen Stress gemacht, um zu feiern?

(f)   Wir haben drei bis vier Tage nur Party gemacht. Außerdem hat die Schule eine große Feier organisiert—mit der ganzen Jahrgangsstufe.

(m)   Und als Belohnung hast du was gemacht?

(f)   Ja, dann sind wir in Urlaub auf die Insel Fuerteventura gefahren. Wir sind eine große Clique von ungefähr zehn Leuten und wir hatten diesen Urlaub schon länger geplant. Es gab viel zu planen—die Flüge, die Unterkunft und die ganzen Unternehmungen—und das war unsere Belohnung für das Abi.

(m)   Wie habt ihr die Reise organisiert?

(f)   Wir haben das per Internet gemacht und haben uns Informationen aus dem Reisebüro geholt.

(m)   Lief alles nach Plan?

(f)   Ja, eigentlich schon. Aber es sind drei Leute verhindert gewesen. Corinna konnte nicht mitgehen—wegen ihrer Eltern. Sie haben es ihr verboten. Mario konnte nicht mit; er hatte eine Arbeit gefunden. Und eine Freundin von mir—Nadine—wurde krank. So konnte auch sie nicht mitgehen. Aber ansonsten lief alles nach Plan.

(m)   Und habt ihr Spaß auf der Insel gehabt?

(f)   Ja, es war cool—super. Wir hatten viel Spaß. Wir sind viel weggegangen. Wir haben am Meer in der Sonne ausgespannt und wir haben eigentlich eine Woche gar nichts gemacht —ein paar Ausflüge am Tag, einige Sehenswürdigkeiten angeschaut—wirklich richtig locker und ohne Stress.

(m) **Ihr habt das Abitur richtig gefeiert, ja? Würdest du das weiterempfehlen?**

(f) Ja, ich würde es auf jeden Fall weiterempfehlen. Es war eine sehr, sehr schöne Zeit. Und die Erholung im Urlaub hat man sich dann richtig verdient. Es ist auch die letzte Gelegenheit, mit den Freunden so viel Zeit zu verbringen, bevor man auf die Uni geht oder eine Arbeit sucht. Und deshalb würde ich es weiterempfehlen, die Zeit einfach zu genießen und viel mit Freunden zu unternehmen.

[END OF TRANSCRIPT]

[BLANK PAGE]

FOR OFFICIAL USE

Examiner's Marks	
A	
B	

Total
Mark

X060/302

NATIONAL
QUALIFICATIONS
2007

WEDNESDAY, 30 MAY
11.00 AM – 12.00 NOON

GERMAN
HIGHER
Listening/Writing

Fill in these boxes and read what is printed below.

Full name of centre

Town

Forename(s)

Surname

Date of birth
Day Month Year   Scottish candidate number   Number of seat

Do not open this paper until told to do so.

Answer Section A **in English** and Section B **in German**.

Section A

Listen carefully to the recording with a view to answering, **in English**, the questions printed in this answer book. Write your answers **clearly** and **legibly** in the spaces provided after each question.

You will have 2 minutes to study the questions before hearing the dialogue for the first time.

The dialogue will be played **twice**, with an interval of 2 minutes between the two playings.

You may make notes at any time but only in this answer book. **Draw your pen through any notes before you hand in the book.**

Move on to Section B when you have completed Section A: you will **not** be told when to do this.

Section B

Do not write your response in this book: **use the 4 page lined answer sheet**.

You will be told to insert the answer sheet inside this book before handing in your work.

You may consult a German dictionary at any time during **both** sections.

Before leaving the examination room you must give this book to the invigilator. If you do not, you may lose all the marks for this paper.

SCOTTISH
QUALIFICATIONS
AUTHORITY

SA X060/302 6/6370

©

Section A

Marks

Nicole, a German-language assistant, is interviewed about her Abitur and what she did after the exams.

1.   What made Nicole's Abitur so stressful?   **2 points**

2.   (*a*) How did she prepare for the exams?   **1 point**

     (*b*) How did this affect her free time?   **2 points**

3.   How did she do in her Abitur?   **1 point**

4.   What celebrations followed the exams?   **2 points**

5.   (*a*) Nicole's reward was a holiday on Fuertaventura. With whom did she go?   **1 point**

     (*b*) What did they have to plan?   **2 points**

Marks

5.   (continued)

(c) How did they go about organising their trip?   **1 point**

6.   In what way did things not quite go according to plan?   **3 points**

7.   How did they spend their time during the holiday?   **3 points**

8.   Why would Nicole recommend doing something like this with friends?   **2 points**

**(20 points)
= 20 marks**

[Turn over for Section B on *Page four*

Marks

Section B

Und du, was hast du vor, diesen Sommer nach den Prüfungen zu machen? Fährst du mit den Eltern oder Freunden in Urlaub oder musst du einen Job finden?

Schreibe 120 – 150 Worte zu diesen Fragen!

10

(30)

USE THE 4 PAGE LINED ANSWER SHEET FOR YOUR ANSWER TO SECTION B

[END OF QUESTION PAPER]

HIGHER

2008

[BLANK PAGE]

X060/301

NATIONAL QUALIFICATIONS 2008	THURSDAY, 5 JUNE 9.00 AM – 10.40 AM	**GERMAN** HIGHER Reading and Directed Writing

45 marks are allocated to this paper. The value attached to each question is shown after each question.

You should spend approximately one hour on Section I and 40 minutes on Section II.

You may use a German dictionary.

SECTION I—READING

Read this magazine article carefully then answer **in English** the questions which follow it.
This article is about a German girl, Sabrina Sadowski, who is spending a year in the United
States as an au pair, living and working in a family.

Zwischen Abenteuer und Wahnsinn

Viele Jugendliche beenden ihre Schulzeit und fragen sich, was sie in Zukunft machen sollen. Studium oder Ausbildung?—wenn studieren, was studieren? Zu Hause bleiben
5 oder ausziehen?—wenn ausziehen, wohin denn? Und einige haben vielleicht gar keine Lust, sofort von der Schule an die Uni zu gehen. Wer würde sich da nicht noch ein Jahr Auszeit wünschen, um sich darüber klar
10 zu werden, was man genau will.

Vor einem Jahr ging es mir nicht anders. Deshalb war mir relativ schnell klar: Ich gehe als Au-pair in die Staaten! Es war die beste Entscheidung, die ich je gemacht habe.
15 Natürlich habe ich Horrorgeschichten über versklavte Au-pairs gehört, aber trotzdem stand ich irgendwann am Flughafen.

Das war vor elf Monaten. Ich habe in dieser Zeit wunderbare Menschen kennen
20 gelernt, zahlreiche neue Dinge erlebt und bin viel selbständiger geworden. Ich habe auch mein Englisch auf ein hohes Niveau bringen können.

Während des Au-pair-Jahres in den Staaten
25 muss man je nach Programm sechs bis zwölf „Credits" sammeln. Diese bekommt man durch einen Collegebesuch, Freiwilligenarbeit oder durch Sprachkurse. Ich zum Beispiel habe einen Erste-Hilfe- und einen
30 Spanischkursus abgeschlossen.

In meiner Familie bin ich für zwei Schulkinder verantwortlich. Daher habe ich jeden Morgen frei. Am Nachmittag bin ich hauptsächlich dazu da, die Kinder zur
35 richtigen Zeit an den richtigen Ort zu bringen und ihnen am Abend etwas zu kochen. Jedes Wochenende und jeden Abend habe ich frei. Unter der Woche treffe ich mich meistens mit Freunden in Cafés,
40 zum Videoabend oder in einer Karaokebar. Am Wochenende erkunden wir New York. Ich lebe mit meiner Gastfamilie in New Jersey. Nach einer knappen Stunde Zugfahrt stehe ich mitten auf dem Broadway in
45 Manhattan.

Aber die Geschichten von Horrorfamilien sind leider nicht alle falsch. So kann es passieren, dass ihr in eine Familie mit zwei hyperaktiven Kindern geratet oder dass eine unfreundliche, junge Leute hassende Oma 50 mit im Haus wohnt. Dass ihr jeden Abend bis 22 Uhr arbeiten müsst, oder dass ihr im Kühlschrank nur bestimmte Dinge essen dürft. Wenn ihr dann abends total fertig, unglücklich und müde in euer Bett fallt, 55 welches sich in einem winzigen Raum unter der Treppe befindet, dann werdet ihr euch doch fragen, wieso ihr dieses Leben mit eurem geliebten Zuhause getauscht habt.

Eine Freundin von mir arbeitet bei einer 60 Familie, wo die Eltern mit ihren Kindern so wenig wie möglich zu tun haben wollen. Jeden Morgen muss sie als erste Aufgabe dem achtjährigen Sohn 70 Tabletten geben und danach das Kind zum Psychiater fahren. 65 Laut dem Psychiater sind die Tabletten nichts als Vitamine!

Es ist fast unmöglich, die „perfekte" Familie zu finden. Hier und da muss man sich anpassen und Regeln akzeptieren. Viele 70 Au-pairs haben unter der Woche „Ausgangssperre". Manche müssen schon um 22 Uhr zu Hause sein. Andere können die ganze Nacht wegbleiben, solange sie am nächsten Morgen wieder da sind, um die 75 Kinder zu wecken.

Familien hier sind so unterschiedlich wie in Deutschland auch. Um die passende Familie zu finden, ist es sinnvoll, so ehrlich wie möglich zu sein und sich ganz genau zu 80 überlegen, was man von dem Jahr erwartet. Bei dem telefonischen Interview mit den Familien hat man die Chance, alle möglichen Fragen zu stellen. Man muss nicht unbedingt für Kinder schwärmen, aber 85 hassen sollte man sie auch nicht gerade.

Ich jedenfalls würde jedem ein solches Jahr empfehlen. Wenn man sich nach dem Motto „Was mich nicht umbringt, macht mich stärker!" in den Flieger setzt, kann kaum 90 etwas schief gehen, und man kann sich auf ein tolles Jahr freuen. Neue Erfahrungen sind zumindest garantiert—positive wie negative.

QUESTIONS

Marks

1. According to paragraph one, what questions might young people ask themselves at the end of their school career?

   2 points

2. Read lines 11–23.

   (*a*) How does Sabrina feel about her choice of going to America as an au pair?

   1 point

   (*b*) Eleven months on, what has been good about the experience?

   Mention **two** things.

   2 points

3. Read lines 24–30.

   (*a*) What can au pairs do to collect the credits required by their programmes?

   Mention **two** things.

   1 point

   (*b*) What has Sabrina chosen?

   1 point

4. Now read lines 31–45.

   (*a*) How does she spend her free time during the week?

   1 point

   (*b*) How is it easy for her to explore New York at the weekend?

   1 point

5. Read lines 46–59.

   (*a*) Some au pairs have unpleasant experiences. Give details of **three** of these.

   3 points

   (*b*) What unpleasant accommodation are some au pairs given?

   1 point

6. Read lines 60–67.

   (*a*) What does she say about the parents her friend worked for?

   1 point

   (*b*) What did her friend have to do each day?

   1 point

7. Read lines 68–76.

   Give details of some of the different rules which au pairs must accept.

   2 points

8. Read lines 77–86.

   What advice does the author give about finding a suitable family?

   1 point

9. Read lines 87–94.

   Why should the au pair adopt the motto "what doesn't kill me will make me stronger"?

   2 points

   (20 points)

   = 20 marks

10. Translate into English:

    „In meiner Familie . . . etwas zu kochen." (lines 31–37)

    10

    (30)

[Turn over for SECTION II on *Page four*

SECTION II—DIRECTED WRITING

Marks

Last summer your parents arranged a house exchange with a German family.

On your return to Scotland, you are asked to write a report **in German** for the website through which the exchange was arranged.

You must include the following information and **you should try to add** other relevant details:

- how you travelled to the house in Germany **and** how you found the journey

- where exactly the house was situated **and** what it was like, compared with your own home

- what your daily routine was, while you were there

- what you did for food throughout your visit

- a family day-trip you went on, while you were in Germany

- whether your family would like to have another house-exchange and why/why not.

Your report should be 150 – 180 words in length.

Marks will be deducted for any area of information that is omitted.　　(15)

[END OF QUESTION PAPER]

X060/303

NATIONAL
QUALIFICATIONS
2008

THURSDAY, 5 JUNE
11.00 AM – 12.00 NOON

GERMAN
HIGHER
Listening Transcript

This paper must not be seen by any candidate.

The material overleaf is provided for use in an emergency only (eg the recording or equipment proving faulty) or where permission has been given in advance by SQA for the material to be read to candidates with additional support needs. The material must be read exactly as printed.

Instructions to reader(s):

The dialogue below should be read in approximately 5 minutes. On completion of the first reading, pause for two minutes, then read the dialogue a second time.

Where special arrangements have been agreed in advance to allow the reading of the material, those sections marked **(m)** should be read by a male speaker and those marked **(f)** by a female.

Candidates have two minutes to study the questions before the transcript is read.

Steffi, a 20 year-old German who is spending a year in Scotland, talks about earlier trips she has made here.

(m) Hatten deine Eltern nichts dagegen, dass du ohne sie nach Schottland fliegst?

(f) Ich bin schon einmal ohne meine Eltern weggefahren. Das hat wunderbar geklappt! Ich glaube, dass meine Eltern mir deshalb bei dieser Reise noch mehr vertrauen!

(m) Was sind die Vorteile, wenn man ohne Eltern wegfährt?

(f) Wenn ich ohne Eltern verreise, bin ich viel freier. Ich kann also mit meinen Freunden bis 3 Uhr morgens feiern gehen und niemand meckert darüber!

Wir konnten auch immer ausschlafen und dann einfach das anschauen, worauf wir Lust hatten.

(m) Woher hast du das Geld für die Reise bekommen?

(f) Ich kriege oft Geld von meinen Verwandten zu meinem Geburtstag. Davon habe ich etwas gespart. Aber ungefähr die Hälfte des Geldes habe ich von meinen Eltern bekommen.

(m) Was musstest du vor der Abfahrt alles organisieren?

(f) Wir mussten natürlich die Flüge buchen und dann noch den Bus zum Flughafen reservieren. Um die Unterkunft haben wir uns auch noch gekümmert. Wir haben uns eine schöne, zentral gelegene Jugendherberge ausgesucht und diese dann im Internet gebucht.

(m) Wie bist du nach Schottland gereist?

(f) Ich habe mich mit meinen Freunden am Hamburger Hauptbahnhof getroffen. Dann sind wir zusammen mit dem Bus zum Flughafen gefahren. Danach sind wir von Hamburg nach Glasgow geflogen.

(m) Gab es irgendwelche Zwischenfälle, als ihr unterwegs wart?

(f) Schon in Hamburg fing der Ärger an! Unser Flugzeug konnte aufgrund des dichten Nebels nicht pünktlich starten. Wir mussten circa eine Stunde warten! Einer meiner Freunde, Thomas, hat am Flughafen auch noch sein Portemonnaie verloren!

(m) Hattet ihr Probleme mit der Unterkunft?

(f) Wir hatten ja ein Zimmer für uns fünf gebucht. Aber als wir in unserer Jugendherberge ankamen, sagten sie uns, dass so ein Zimmer nicht mehr frei wäre. Wir haben jedoch ganz schnell eine neue, schöne Jugendherberge gefunden.

(m) Gab es Freizeitmöglichkeiten in der Jugendherberge?

(f) Es gab einen großen Billardraum und im Wohnzimmer gab es viele Spiele und Bücher, die man benutzen konnte. Im kleinen Garten stand sogar ein Grill. Wenn es nicht geregnet hat, haben wir einen gemütlichen Abend draußen verbracht.

(m) Was hast du alles in Glasgow unternommen?

(f) In Glasgow haben wir uns zum Beispiel die Kunstgalerie angesehen. Einkaufen waren wir natürlich auch, die Innenstadt hat ja so viele Geschäfte! Außerdem gibt es in Glasgow eine so große Auswahl an Klubs und Kneipen.

(m) Warst du nur in Glasgow?

(f) Nein, nach ein paar Tagen in Glasgow sind wir nach Edinburgh gefahren. Wir haben uns die bekannte Burg angeschaut und sind die Princes Street entlang geschlendert. Dann führte uns unsere Reise in den Norden. Es ging nach Fort William und dort sind wir wandern gegangen.

(m) Würdest du Schottland als Reiseziel empfehlen?

(f) Schottland ist auf jeden Fall eine Reise wert. Die Städte haben ein reiches Kulturangebot, ein aufregendes Nachtleben und sehr gute Einkaufsmöglichkeiten! Gleichzeitig kann man in Schottland eine wunderbare Natur erleben—die vielen Seen und das Hochland sind sehr sehenswert.

(m) Warst du zum ersten Mal in Großbritannien?

(f) Nein. In der 7. Klasse sind wir nach Inverness gereist. Unsere Schule in Hamburg und die in Inverness haben ein Austauschprogramm. In einem Jahr kommen die schottischen Schüler nach Hamburg und im nächsten Jahr fliegen die deutschen Jugendlichen nach Inverness. Das ist eine tolle Möglichkeit ein neues Land kennen zu lernen.

(m) Würdest du eine Auslandserfahrung, wie diese Reise nach Schottland, anderen Jugendlichen weiter empfehlen?

(f) Ich würde diesen Trip auf jeden Fall weiter empfehlen! Wir haben neue Menschen und eine andere, spannende Kultur kennen gelernt! Es hat uns allen richtig viel Spaß gemacht!

[END OF TRANSCRIPT]

[BLANK PAGE]

FOR OFFICIAL USE

Examiner's Marks	
A	
B	

Total Mark

X060/302

NATIONAL
QUALIFICATIONS
2008

THURSDAY, 5 JUNE
11.00 AM – 12.00 NOON

GERMAN
HIGHER
Listening/Writing

Fill in these boxes and read what is printed below.

Full name of centre

Town

Forename(s)

Surname

Date of birth

Day Month Year   Scottish candidate number   Number of seat

Do not open this paper until told to do so.

Answer Section A **in English** and Section B **in German**.

Section A

Listen carefully to the recording with a view to answering, **in English**, the questions printed in this answer book. Write your answers **clearly and legibly** in the spaces provided after each question.

You will have 2 minutes to study the questions before hearing the dialogue for the first time.

The dialogue will be played **twice**, with an interval of 2 minutes between the two playings.

You may make notes at any time but only in this answer book. **Draw your pen through any notes before you hand in the book.**

Move on to Section B when you have completed Section A: you will **not** be told when to do this.

Section B

Do not write your response in this book: **use the 4 page lined answer sheet**.

You will be told to insert the answer sheet inside this book before handing in your work.

You may consult a German dictionary at any time during **both** sections.

Before leaving the examination room you must give this book to the invigilator. If you do not, you may lose all the marks for this paper.

DO NOT
WRITE
THIS
MARGI

Section A

Marks

Steffi, a 20 year-old German who is spending a year in Scotland, talks about earlier trips she has made here.

1. What are the advantages of going on holiday without your parents?   **3 points**

2. How **exactly** did she get the money for the holiday?   **2 points**

3. What **three** things did they have to organise before leaving?   **3 points**

4. What went wrong before they even left Hamburg?   **2 points**

5. What difficulty did they have with their accommodation?   **1 point**

Marks

6. What facilities did their accommodation have?   **2 points**

7. Why did they enjoy shopping in Glasgow?   **1 point**

8. What did they do in Edinburgh?   **1 point**

9. What does she say about Scotland as a tourist destination?   Give **two** details.   **2 points**

10. What information does she give about her first visit to Scotland?   **2 points**

11. Why would Steffi recommend a trip abroad?   **1 point**

**(20 points)
= 20 marks**

[Turn over for Section B on *Page four*

Marks

Section B

Und du, würdest du mit Freunden, mit der Familie oder alleine verreisen? Welche Art von Urlaub sagt dir zu—zum Beispiel Relaxen am Meer oder durch Europa reisen?

Schreibe 120 – 150 Worte zu diesen Fragen!

10

(30)

USE THE 4 PAGE LINED ANSWER SHEET FOR YOUR ANSWER TO SECTION B

[END OF QUESTION PAPER]

HIGHER

2009

[BLANK PAGE]

X060/301

NATIONAL
QUALIFICATIONS
2009

WEDNESDAY, 20 MAY
1.00 PM – 2.40 PM

GERMAN
HIGHER
Reading and
Directed Writing

45 marks are allocated to this paper. The value attached to each question is shown after each question.

You should spend approximately one hour on Section I and 40 minutes on Section II.

You may use a German dictionary.

SECTION I—READING

Read the whole of this newspaper article carefully and then answer **in English** the questions which follow it.

Three generations of a German family write about their experiences of summer. Grandmother Ingrid Dehnert (65) and mother Katrin Bredner (43) compare with daughter Carolin (17) how summer was then and what it is like now.

Von Limo zu Tequila Sunrise

Das, was die Menschen am Sommer genießen, scheint sich im Laufe der Zeit nicht geändert zu haben. Sonne, Wärme und Freizeit sind auch für diese drei Frauen die
5 absolut besten Dinge an der sommerlichen Jahreszeit. Wie man die freie Zeit jedoch nutzt, das hat sich mit jeder Generation stark verändert.

Ferienbeschäftigung

10 „Als ich noch jung war, machte ich in der Sommerzeit immer viel mit Freunden zusammen. Wir gingen viel baden, mussten aber immer laufen, da es noch keine Busse gab. Ich arbeitete nebenbei auch als
15 Kindermädchen und verdiente am Tag 50 Pfennige und eine Buttersemmel", berichtet Oma Ingrid Dehnert. „Wir haben auch immer die Touristen von der Fähre abgeholt und ihre Koffer in die Pensionen
20 gefahren. Wir sind aber nie in den Urlaub gefahren, weil wir nicht genug Geld hatten. Meine Mutter sagte oft zu uns Kindern: ‚Ich möchte so gerne einmal mit euch in die Berge fahren . . .!' Sie wollte uns immer die
25 Alpen zeigen."

In der Generation von Mutter Katrin Bredner war es schon anders: „Ich habe ab und zu in der Milchbar gearbeitet, bin sehr viel wandern gegangen, und manchmal sind
30 wir auch in den Urlaub an die Ostsee gefahren."

Tochter Carolin erzählt: „Heute gehen wir viel in die Disco, auf Open-Air-Konzerte, ins Kino und Döner, Pizza oder Eis essen."

35 ### Essen und Trinken

„Egal, wo wir hingegangen sind, wir haben unser Essen mitgenommen. Wenn wir das Geld hatten, haben wir eine Flasche Limonade gekauft, die wir uns geteilt
40 haben", erzählt Oma Ingrid. Die Getränke des Sommers haben sich im Laufe der Zeit stark geändert. Von Limonade bis Cola war es ein langer Weg. Heute stehen Mixgetränke wie Tequila Sunrise oder Cosmopolitan auf der Getränkekarte. 45

Sommermode

Auch in Sachen Kleidung passierte ein großer Wandel. „Früher hatten wir noch selbst geschneiderte Sachen. Wir trugen in der Regel Kleider und Röcke. Außerdem 50 krempelten wir die Röcke hoch, um Miniröcke zu erhalten. Meine Lieblingsfarbe des Sommers war damals Rot", sagt die Großmutter.

„In unserer Zeit gab es schon Miniröcke, 55 aber auch kurze Hosen. Die Farbe des Sommers war damals Blau", so Katrin Bredner. Carolin Bredner weiß, wie es jetzt aussieht: „Heute sind viele Farben aktuell. Auch Streifen werden oft getragen", sagt sie. 60

Party und Feiern

Neben der Mode sind noch weitere Unterschiede festzustellen. Viele Jugendliche in der heutigen Zeit nutzen die Ferien, um richtig zu feiern. Daran war früher 65 nicht zu denken. In der Generation von Ingrid Dehnert waren die einzigen Feiermöglichkeiten Familienfeste, und selbst dann mussten die Kinder um Mitternacht zu Hause sein. Katrin Bredner dagegen lebt in 70 einer Generation, die in ihrer Jugend schon viel die Disco besuchte. Heute ist es am extremsten. „Wir gehen heute, wenn es klappt, jedes Wochenende in die Disco. Jugendliche besuchen auch Stadtfeste zum 75 Feiern", erklärt Carolin.

Musik und Sommerhits

Die spannendste Verwandlung passierte jedoch bei der Musik. Als Oma Ingrid noch jung war, wurden nur Wanderlieder 80 gesungen. Jedoch in der Generation von Katrin Bredner war das schon ganz anders. Die Jugendlichen nahmen ihre eigenen Stimmen und viel Musik mit einem Kassettenrekorder auf und hörten sich diese 85 an. Heute kommt nahezu kein Jugendlicher ohne MP3-Player oder I-Pod aus.

Fazit

Zum Schluss sollen die drei Frauen den
90 Satz „Ich habe den Sommer in meiner Jugend genossen, weil . . ." fortsetzen.

„. . . weil man Freizeit hat und die Sonne und die Ruhe genießen kann", antwortet Carolin Bredner. Ihre Mutter Katrin sagt: „. . . weil mir die Sonne sehr wichtig war und 95 man sich entspannen konnte." Die Antwort von Oma Ingrid ist jedoch die, die am meisten fasziniert. „Wir waren frei", sagt sie.

QUESTIONS

Marks

1. (a) Across the three generations, what has **not** changed over the years? **1 point**

   (b) What has changed a great deal? **1 point**

2. Read lines 9–34.

   (a) What does grandmother Ingrid Dehnert say about going swimming with friends in summer, when she was young? **1 point**

   (b) Apart from child-minding, what did she do to earn money? **2 points**

   (c) How did Katrin Bredner spend her holidays? **2 points**

3. Read lines 35–45.

   In grandmother Ingrid's day, what did they do for food and drink, when they went out? **2 points**

4. Now read lines 46–60.

   (a) What sort of clothes did grandmother Ingrid's generation wear in the summer? **1 point**

   (b) What does Katrin say about clothes in her day? **1 point**

   (c) What do today's young people wear? **1 point**

5. Read lines 61–76.

   (a) What are you told about parties, when Ingrid was young? **2 points**

   (b) How do the young people of today like to celebrate? **2 points**

6. Read lines 77–87.

   What changes in music took place between Oma Ingrid's and Katrin Bredner's generation? **2 points**

7. Read lines 88–98.

   Why did Katrin enjoy summers, when she was a girl? **2 points**

   (20 points)

   = 20 marks

8. Translate into English:

   „Wir sind aber . . . uns immer die Alpen zeigen." (lines 20–25) **10**

   (30)

[Turn over for SECTION II on *Page four*

SECTION II—DIRECTED WRITING

Marks

You have travelled to Germany to spend three months working in a town there.

When you return to Scotland, you have to write a report **in German** for the languages department in your school/college.

You must include the following information and **you should try to add** other relevant details:

*   how you travelled to Germany **and** what the town was like

*   where your accommodation was situated **and** what it was like

*   what your job involved **and** how you got on with the people you worked with

*   what you did in your spare time to experience the country/culture

*   what you did on your last night before coming home

*   why you would/would not recommend working in Germany to others.

Your report should be 150 – 180 words in length.

Marks will be deducted for any area of information that is omitted.   **(15)**

[END OF QUESTION PAPER]

X060/303

NATIONAL QUALIFICATIONS 2009	WEDNESDAY, 20 MAY 3.00 PM – 4.00 PM	GERMAN HIGHER Listening Transcript

This paper must not be seen by any candidate.

The material overleaf is provided for use in an emergency only (eg the recording or equipment proving faulty) or where permission has been given in advance by SQA for the material to be read to candidates with additional support needs. The material must be read exactly as printed.

Instructions to reader(s):

The dialogue below should be read in approximately 3½ minutes. On completion of the first reading, pause for two minutes, then read the dialogue a second time.

Where special arrangements have been agreed in advance to allow the reading of the material, those sections marked **(m)** should be read by a male speaker and those marked **(f)** by a female.

Candidates have two minutes to study the questions before the transcript is read.

Meike, a 20 year-old German from Markersdorf near Görlitz in Saxony, talks about getting a training place.

(m) Meike, wo kommst du her und wo wohnst du jetzt?

(f)   Ich komme aus Markersdorf. Das ist eine Gemeinde in Sachsen mit etwa 4.500 Einwohnern. Jetzt wohne ich in Hamburg, das ist eine Großstadt und liegt etwa 500 km von Görlitz entfernt.

(m) Warum bist du nach Hamburg gezogen?

(f)   Hier in Görlitz gibt es nur relativ wenige Ausbildungsplätze für die vielen Schüler. Für uns gibt es nur eine einzige Alternative. Wir müssen unsere Stadt, Eltern und Freunde verlassen, um in einer anderen Stadt einen Ausbildungsplatz zu bekommen. Deswegen bin ich nach Hamburg gezogen.

(m) Wie war das am Anfang?

(f)   Nicht so einfach. Natürlich habe ich meine Freunde, meine Familie und meine Umgebung vermisst. Am Anfang kennt man ja niemanden. Mittlerweile habe ich schon viele Freunde gefunden.

(m) Gibt es Vorteile, wenn man weit weg von zu Hause wohnt?

(f)   Selbstverständlich! Man kann Freunde mit nach Hause bringen - egal wie spät es ist. Und am Wochenende kann man solange schlafen, wie man will.

(m) Gibt es auch Nachteile?

(f)   Na klar. Man muss alles selbst machen. Das bedeutet, man muss selbst einkaufen, selbst putzen und sich sein Geld einteilen, damit es bis zum Ende des Monats reicht.

(m) Wolltest du von zu Hause wegziehen?

(f)   Eigentlich, ja. Für mich war es eine gute Entscheidung, fortzugehen. Im Vergleich zu meinen alten Klassenkameraden und Freunden, die in Görlitz arbeiten, verdiene ich auch mehr Geld.

(m) Wie hast du diese Ausbildungsstelle in Hamburg bekommen?

(f)   Eigentlich nur durch Zufall! Ein Arbeitskollege ist krank geworden und ich habe seinen Platz bekommen. Ich war recht froh, diese Stelle in Hamburg zu bekommen, weil ich in Norddeutschland leben wollte.

(m) Wie ist es mit dem Umzug nach Hamburg gelaufen?

(f)   Ich hatte das Glück, dass meine Eltern mich beim Umzug sehr unterstützt haben. Sie haben mir sehr viel geholfen. Sie sind mit mir zusammen nach Hamburg gefahren und wir haben eine Wohnung gesucht. Innerhalb von drei Tagen haben sie mit mir alles für die Wohnung gekauft.

(m) **Ist es wirklich ein großer Unterschied, ob man in Hamburg oder in Görlitz lebt?**

(f) Ja, das sowieso. Hamburg ist nicht nur sehr viel größer, die Einwohner sprechen auch einen anderen Dialekt.

(m) **Fährst du noch oft nach Görlitz?**

(f) Nicht so oft. Aber ich bin froh, wenn ich mal wieder zu Hause bin, weil ich dann meine alten Freunde treffen kann.

(m) **War es für dich ein sehr großer Schritt von zu Hause auszuziehen?**

(f) Sicher. Seitdem ich in Hamburg wohne, bin ich auf jeden Fall selbstständiger geworden und vielleicht sogar ein Stück erwachsener.

[END OF TRANSCRIPT]

[BLANK PAGE]

FOR OFFICIAL USE

Examiner's Marks

A	
B	

Total Mark

X060/302

NATIONAL
QUALIFICATIONS
2009

WEDNESDAY, 20 MAY
3.00 PM – 4.00 PM

GERMAN
HIGHER
Listening/Writing

Fill in these boxes and read what is printed below.

Full name of centre

Town

Forename(s)

Surname

Date of birth

Day   Month   Year   Scottish candidate number   Number of seat

Do not open this paper until told to do so.

Answer Section A **in English** and Section B **in German**.

Section A

Listen carefully to the recording with a view to answering, **in English**, the questions printed in this answer book. Write your answers **clearly and legibly** in the spaces provided after each question.

You will have 2 minutes to study the questions before hearing the dialogue for the first time.

The dialogue will be played **twice**, with an interval of 2 minutes between the two playings.

You may make notes at any time but only in this answer book. **Score out any notes before you hand in the book.**

Move on to Section B when you have completed Section A: you will **not** be told when to do this.

Section B

Do not write your response in this book: **use the 4 page lined answer sheet**.

You will be told to insert the answer sheet inside this book before handing in your work.

You may consult a German dictionary at any time during **both** sections.

Before leaving the examination room you must give this book to the invigilator. If you do not, you may lose all the marks for this paper.

Section A

Marks

Meike, a 20 year-old German from Markersdorf near Görlitz in Saxony, talks about getting a training place.

1. How many people live in Markersdorf?   **1 point**

2. (*a*) What does Meike say about the number of training places in Görlitz?   **1 point**

    (*b*) What is the only alternative the young people have?   **1 point**

3. At the beginning, how did she find living in Hamburg?   **2 points**

4. What are the advantages of living far away from home?   **2 points**

5. What are the disadvantages?   **3 points**

6. Why does she feel that moving away was a good decision?   **1 point**

Marks

7. (*a*) How did Meike get this training place?   **1 point**

(*b*) Why was she pleased?   **1 point**

8. How did her parents help her with the move to Hamburg?   **3 points**

9. What are the **two** differences between Hamburg and Görlitz?   **2 points**

10. Why does she like to go back to Görlitz?   **1 point**

11. How has she changed since leaving home?   **1 point**

(20 points)
= 20 marks

[Turn over for Section B on *Page four*

Marks

Section B

Was meinst du, was sind die Vorteile und Nachteile von deinem Wohnort? Willst du lieber bei den Eltern wohnen oder von Zuhause ausziehen?

Schreibe 120 – 150 Worte zu diesen Fragen!

10

(30)

USE THE 4 PAGE LINED ANSWER SHEET FOR YOUR ANSWER TO SECTION B

[END OF QUESTION PAPER]

[BLANK PAGE]

[BLANK PAGE]

[BLANK PAGE]

[BLANK PAGE]

[BLANK PAGE]

[BLANK PAGE]

Acknowledgements

Permission has been sought from all relevant copyright holders and Bright Red Publishing is grateful for the use of the following:

An article by Katja Bub is taken from the newspaper 'Hersbrucker Zeitung', 10 July 2004 © Hersbrucker Zeitung (2006 Reading & Directed Writing pages 2 & 3);

An article by Sabrina Sodowski taken from the newspaper 'Kolner Stadt-Anzeiger' © Kolner Stadt-Anzeiger (2008 Reading & Directed Writing pages 2 & 3);

The article 'Von Limo zu Sex on the Beach' by Florian Thalmann taken from the newspaper 'Sachsische Zeiturg', Jurge Szene, 16th August 2007 © Sachsische Zeitung GmbH (2009 Reading & Directed Writing pages 2&3).

SQA HIGHER GERMAN
2006–2009

SECTION I – READING

1. *Any two from:*
   - their life is expensive
     being a student/a young person is expensive
     they need money for: 2 ex their phone, clothes, the cinema, holidays
   - pocket money (usually) not enough
     pocket money does not cover their costs
     the money they get from their parents is not enough/insufficient/inadequate
   - so that they do not have to rely on parents
     so that they can earn their own money
     so that they do not need to go to their parents
     it is a welcome alternative to the parental purse
     to stop taking money from their parent's purse/pocket

2. (a) • delivers/distributes <u>TV (guides) and other magazines/illustrated papers</u> **or**
     delivers/distributes magazines/papers/does a paper-round <u>twice a week</u> **or**
     delivers/distributes magazines/papers/does a paper-round <u>on his bike</u>
   (b) • <u>exchange/school</u>-trip to France <u>and</u> trip/journey/holiday/travel to Scotland
   (c) • mother saw/read advert in the paper
     mother found the job/it in the paper
     mother showed him the ad in the paper
     his mum read about it in the newspaper

3. (a) • divides his round into 3
     divides the area into 3 rounds
     does it in 3 trips
     he shares it between 3 tours
     in 3 tours of the district
   • does one round after the other (on his bike)
     does each in turn

3. (b) • has to go out in all weathers/no matter the weather/he has to work in any weather conditions
     customers want their magazines in all weathers/despite the weather
     or
   • it is awful/difficult/bad/not good/rubbish/silly/stupid/a pain when it is hot/there is (black) ice
     it seems stupid when it is hot/there is (black) ice
   (c) *Any two from:*
     • easy money
     • fun/likes doing it/enjoys his job
     • does not interfere with his school work/school work does not suffer/school work can fit around it

4. (a) • financial independence/freedom
     she was financially dependent/she is financially independent
   (b) • because of the hourly rate/pay/wages <u>and</u> tips
     good pay <u>and</u> tips

5. *Any two from:*
   • every customer/guest is different/the work is varied
   • she finds working/dealing/getting on with people easy/the contact with people is easy for her
     she finds it easy to relate to people
   • you learn to approach people in a relaxed way
     you learn to be relaxed with/around/towards people
     you learn to be cool with people
   • (you learn) to be friendly/nice/pleasant towards unfriendly/unkind people/guests/customers/clients
   • some days/sometimes/at times/there are days when it is/can be stressful/can cause a lot of stress

6. (a) • because of her school leaving/end of school/final exams
     so her work doesn't affect her marks/grades/results/exams
     she does not want her school grades affected
     so she does not spoil her school grades
     so that work does not impair/get in the way of her school grades
     she has to concentrate on her grades
     to get the grades she wants
     to get her grades

6. (b) • she's improved her mental arithmetic
     she is better at mental arithmetic/sums in her head/working things out in her head/counting in her head/calculating in her head
     with mental arithmetic

7. (a) *Any two from:*
     • direct contact with the public/customers
     • fills/stacks the shelves/fills the empty shelves
     • <u>in charge of/responsible for</u> the empties in the drinks department
   (b) *Any two from:*
     • <u>it's good/nice</u> he is earning money
       <u>they are pleased</u> he is earning money
     • his brother did same job before/once/earlier
       his brother had the/this/that job
     • there have been no problems with school
       it did not affect his/their schooling
       the job gave his brother no problems with school

8. *Any one from:*
   • you have a different/new attitude towards money
     you have a different feel(ing) for money
     you feel differently about money
     you have another feeling for money
     you get a new feeling for money
     you get a better understanding of money
     you get a better sense about money

8. *continued*

> you get a different outlook on money
> it has given him an appreciation of the value of money

- you think about/consider how you spend your money/what you spend it on/what you buy with it
  you spend it in a more considered way
  you are <u>more</u> careful with money/you take <u>more</u> care with money
- he would not want to do this for ever/life
  he would not want to do this job all his life/his whole life

9. ,,Ich weiβ genau, wo man alles im Supermarkt finden kann"

I know exactly/precisely/the exact place where you can find/one/people can find everything in the supermarket/all the things in the supermarket/anything in the supermarket/where everything can be found in the supermarket

und welche Flaschen wir zurücknehmen dürfen, sagt Andreas.

and which/what bottles we are allowed/permitted to/may take back/accept says/said Andreas.

Wenn Kunden genervt und unfreundlich sind,

If/When/Whenever customers/clients are irritated/worked up/annoyed/stressed and unfriendly/unpleasant

hat er seine eigene Taktik entwickelt:

he has developed/he has worked out/he has devised/ his own strategy/strategies/tactics/tactic

Man muss sympathisch sein und den Kunden helfen.

You/One must be/have to be/need to be pleasant/nice/ congenial and help the customers/clients/be helpful to the customers/provide help for the customers.

SECTION II – DIRECTED WRITING

Please see the table on pages 9–10 which provides details of the criteria required to produce a good essay answer.

SECTION A

1. •   so that they are healthy/healthier/fit when they are older/old/adults/in later life/in the future
so that they aren't unhealthy when they are older

2. *Any two from:*
- goes jogging/running <u>with friend(s)</u> **or**
  goes jogging/running <u>regularly</u>
- gets/goes to/takes badminton <u>lessons</u>
- plays volleyball <u>twice a week</u>

3. •   would/does not go to McDonalds/fast food restaurants <u>every day/daily</u>
does not go to McDonalds <u>much/regularly/very often</u>
does not eat fast food <u>every day</u>
<u>rarely/seldom</u> eats fast food/McDonalds
does not eat <u>much/a lot of</u> fast food
would/does not <u>live off</u> fast food
<u>avoids/keeps clear of</u> fast food
eats <u>a limited amount</u> of fast food
- eats <u>a lot/plenty of</u> salad and vegetables

4. •   few(er)/not (as/so) many/less/not a lot of Germans go to fast food restaurants
- Scotland/Britain/here – (lots of) <u>families with young/small/little children</u> eat/live on fast food/go there
  <u>young families</u> go there

5. •   (a lot of) fruit <u>each/every day/daily</u>
- <u>not too/so many/much/not a lot of</u> sweets/sweeties/ candy/confectionery

6. •   sometimes   + <u>at the weekend</u>
now and again/then
from time to time
occasionally
not very often
not regularly
every so often

some weekends

7. (*a*) •   there is a problem in <u>cities/big(ger) towns/in the city</u>
no more or less than in Scotland
it is much the same as in Scotland
no better or worse than in Scotland
it is pretty much equal to Scotland
not any great difference between Scotland and Germany

(*b*) •   can drink/buy <u>beer or wine at 16</u> (in pub)
- can buy it in shop at 16

8. *Any two from:*
- it is unhealthy/bad for your health
  it is bad for you
- she does not smoke/never has smoked (and never will)

- (lots of) young people/teenagers do it because it is/looks cool
  young people do it to look cool
- people smoke due to peer pressure

9. • a lot of/(too) many people are too fat
   a lot of people have health problems because of weight/they are fat
- little/small/young children who are very/really/too fat/really overweight/obese
  there are (some) very fat small children
  some small children are very fat
  little/small/young children who cannot/are unable to do sport because of their size/because they are so fat

10. *Any three from:*
- German children/they eat a sandwich/bread (and butter)/roll/apple at the interval/at break
  Germans take a sandwich to school
- sweets not sold in schools (in Germany)
  you cannot buy sweets in schools
- Scots eat crisps at break time/at school
  In Scotland they eat crisps at break time/at school
  Germans do not eat crisps at school
- (German) children do sport in the afternoon/after school/after lunch
  almost every German child does sport
  lots of sports clubs for them

SECTION B

Please see the table on pages 12-13 which provides details of the criteria required to produce a good essay answer.

HIGHER GERMAN READING AND DIRECTED WRITING 2007

SECTION I—READING

1. (*a*) He worked on a farm in Australia (in 2001)
   (*b*) *Any two from:*
- It is cramped/limited/crowded/packed/enclosed/not open enough/restricting/constricting/claustrophobic/limiting
  he feels confined and closed in/it feels too small
- too much stress/too stressful
- too much pressure to succeed/achieve/perform/work hard/do well
   (*c*) when the children are older/grown-up/adults
   when the children grow up

2. (*a*) • with her qualifications she has/will have...
   ...good prospects/opportunities/chances in Australia
   ...a good chance of succeeding/doing well/getting a job in Australia
   ...a good/greater/better chance in Australia
   Her qualifications as a nurse could be wanted in Australia
- her daughter can/could start school at (age of) four
  in a year her daughter will be able to start school in Australia
   (*b*) • she does not have the money/the 2000 dollars...
   ...for a visa and the test she'd have to sit
   the cost/expense of the visa and test she would have to sit

3. *Any two from:*
- it/you can/could/might be lonely
  it is sometimes lonely
- (when you are) sitting quietly/silently in a corner
- you cannot understand jokes/one joke in English
- to speak to Australians you need to know/learn about Australian/their politics/sport/humour

4. (*a*) • high cost and time needed to return to Germany
   it costs/takes a lot of time and money to go/get back to Germany/to visit Germany
   it costs/takes a lot of time and money to come (back) from Australia
   (*b*) *Any three of*
- often works six days a week
- has never worked so hard/so long/such long hours in his life
- no lunch/dinner/midday break even in 40 degree heat
- pay/wages/money/salary is less than in Germany/at home
  wages are low compared with Germany

5. (a) • the smell of smoke/it smells of smoke
   • the laugh/call/cry/shriek/scream of the kookaburra/a bird
   (b) • met and married Marcel
      met her husband
      met someone and got married
   (c) • their openness/they are (very) open
      it is easy to get to know them/make contact with them
      you make acquaintances quickly
      you make/form contacts quickly

6. (a) • the school system is not so/very good
      good schools are generally/mostly/usually/normally/mainly/(very) often/predominantly/as a rule private and expensive
   (b) • she wants her children to go to school in Germany/a German school
      • Antje will/wants to take over/take on/run her parents' business/firm/company in Berlin

7. Gerhard Scheller hat seinen deutschen Pass abgegeben
   Gerhard Scheller has given up/in/back gave up/in/back has handed in/over/back/handed in/over/back his German passport

   und ist jetzt stolz darauf, australischer Staatsbürger zu sein.
   and is now proud of/about being/to be an Australian citizen/an Australian national

   Gerhard und seine Frau Britta haben sich kennen gelernt
   Gerhard and his wife Britta met/got to know each/one other/came to know each other

   als sie in Hamburg Informatik studierten.
   when/whilst they studied/did/they were studying/doing computing science/computer science/IT/Information Technology/Information Systems/Information Science in Hamburg.

   Seit 1994 leben sie in einem Vorort von Sydney.
   Since 1994 they have been living/they have lived in a suburb of Sydney/Sydney suburb.

SECTION II – DIRECTED WRITING

Please see the table on pages 9–10 which provides details of the criteria required to produce a good essay answer.

SECTION A

1. *Any two from:*
   • a lot/lots/(so) much/loads/a huge amount to learn/study/do/revise
      she had so much work to do for them
   • a lot of/lots of/loads of/(so) many <u>books</u> to read
      she had to study from many books
   • essays to write

2. (a) • She had a revision/study/learning plan/programme
         She made a timetable for learning/a revision timetable
         or
      • She studied/learned new/different things/stuff/topics each week
         She studied something else/new things each week
   (b) *Any two from:*
      • She did not have any (free time)/She had none.
         No (more) free time.
         It took away her free time
         Her time was all taken up
      • Could not see/meet/go out with her friends as/so often/as/so much
      • Hardly any time for sport
         Practically/almost no time for sport
         She did hardly any sport

3. • She was pleased/happy/satisfied/content with her mark(s)/grade(s)/result(s)
      She thought she had done very well
      or
   • she got (an average of) 1.5

4. • 3 to 4 days/3 or 4 days of parties/partying
      They had a party/partied for 3 or 4 days/3 to 4 days
      There was a 3-4 day party
   • (People from) school organised/had/held/threw/arranged (big)"do"/event/party/celebration/dance/ceremony

5. (a) a big/large group/crowd/clique of friends/pals
      (about) 10 friends/pals
      10 of her friends/pals
   (b) *Any two from:*
      • the flight(s)/plane(s)
         the plane journey/ticket(s)
      • accommodation/somewhere to stay
         where to spend the night
      • activities
         what (they were going) to do
         everything/things to do

   (c) • internet/websites <u>and</u> travel agent/bureau/office
         booked it on-line <u>and</u> got info from the travel agent

6. *Any three from:*
- three of the group could not go/make it
  three people pulled out
- one – could not go because of parents
  one – because of her parents/because her parents banned her
  Corinna's parents would not let her go
  Corinna was not allowed to go
- one – could not go because of work
  Mario found/got a job/had to work
- one – could not go because of illness
  Nadine took ill

7. *Any three from:*
- went out a lot
- relaxing by the sea/on the beach
  relaxing in the sun
  by the sea in the sun
  (Answer must have 2 elements of relax+sea+sun.)
- spent a week doing nothing (at all)
- went on a couple/few/some excursions/
  (day-) trips/outings
- did some sightseeing
  saw the sights
  went to see the sights

8.
- last chance/opportunity/time to spend time with/to be with/to see your friends
- before going to university or starting a job
  before university or work/job.

SECTION B

Please see the table on pages 12–13 which provides details of the criteria required to produce a good essay answer.

HIGHER GERMAN READING AND DIRECTED WRITING 2008

SECTION I – READING

1.
- study/studies/college/university or apprenticeship/ train(ing)/further education/become a trainee/learn a trade <u>and</u> (if study), what (to study)
- stay at home or move out/take off/leave (your house/ home)/go elsewhere <u>and</u> (if move out), where (to)

2. *(a)*
- it was the best decision ever/so far/yet
  it was the best decision she ever made

(b) Any two from:
- she has met/got to know wonderful/great/ marvellous people
- she has experienced (so) many/countless/ numerous/a large number of/a lot of new things
  she has had so many new experiences
- she has become/she is (now) <u>much more</u> independent/<u>really</u> independent
- she has brought/taken/got her English up to a high/advanced level/standard

3. *(a) Any two from:*
- attend/go to college
- voluntary/charity work
- language class/course

(b) • a first-aid course <u>and</u> a Spanish course

4. *(a)*
- meets friends in cafés, to watch videos/films/for a video/film evening/movie-night or in a karaoke bar

(b)
- it only takes (about) an hour/it takes (just) under an hour in the train to get to New York/Manhattan (from where she stays/New Jersey)

5. *(a) Any three from:*
- <u>family</u> with <u>two</u> hyperactive children
  some families have 2 hyperactive children
- unfriendly granny lives in the house
  granny who hates young people lives in the house
- <u>have to/must</u> work until 10.00 pm/22.00 <u>every night</u>
- only allowed to eat certain things/particular food from the fridge
  not allowed particular things to eat from the fridge

(b) • tiny/small/little room under the stairs

6. *(a)* • they wanted as little as possible to do with their child(ren)

(b) • give the 8 year old (boy/son) 70 tablets and/then take the boy/child to the psychiatrist

7. *Any two from:*
- not allowed out during the week/on week-days
  cannot go out during the week/on week-days
  are banned from going out during the week/on week-days
  have a going out ban during the week/on week-days

7. *continued*
- (must) be in/home at/before/by 10.00 pm/22.00
  have a curfew to be in at 10
  have a 10 pm curfew
- can stay out/away all night as long as they are back/in/home (in time) to waken children
  can stay out all night as long as they wake up the children

8. *Any one from:*
- be as honest/genuine/truthful as possible
- think carefully/exactly about what you/to want/expect from the year
  consider what you want from the year
- ask all your questions during the telephone interview
  use a/the telephone interview as an opportunity to put questions to the family
  use the telephone interview and ask questions
  have a telephone interview and ask about things

9. *Any two from:*
- if that is your attitude/in this mind set/in that case/if you do,/(because) then hardly anything can go wrong
- you <u>can</u> <u>look forward</u> to a great/brilliant/fantastic/super/mad year
- new experiences are guaranteed - positive/good as well as/and/or negative/bad

10. In meiner Familie bin ich für zwei Schulkinder verantwortlich.
In my family I am responsible for/in charge of two school-children/school-kids/children of school age

Daher habe ich jeden Morgen frei.
Because of this/that/For this/that reason/So/That's why/Therefore/Hence/This/That means/Due to that I have every morning/the morning/(the) mornings/in the morning(s) off/free.
That's why I am off/free every morning.

Am Nachmittag bin ich hauptsächlich dazu da,
In the afternoon(s) I am mainly/chiefly here/there
In the afternoon the main reason I am there is

die Kinder zur richtigen Zeit an den richtigen Ort zu bringen
to bring/of bringing/(I) bring/to take/of taking/(I) take/to get/of getting/(I) get the children to the right/correct/proper place at the right/correct/proper time

und ihnen am Abend etwas zu kochen.
and (to) cook/cooking/(I) cook something for them/them something (to eat) in the evening(s).

SECTION II – DIRECTED WRITING

Please see the table on pages 9–10 which provides details of the criteria required to produce a good essay answer.

SECTION A

1. *Any three from:*
- (much) more freedom/freer/more free/more independent
- can party/celebrate/stay out (with friends) until 3.00 am/the early morning/early in the morning
  can come in at 3.00 am/early in the morning
- nobody can moan/complain about this/it
- can have a long lie/stay in bed late/lie in/sleep as long as you want
  can wake/get up when you want
  do not have to get up early
- can (go and) see/look at what(ever) you want

2. • <u>birthday</u> money from <u>relatives</u>
  or
  <u>saved</u> her <u>birthday</u> money
- <u>half</u> the money came from <u>parents</u>

3. • (book) flights/flight reservation/plane tickets/plane from Hamburg/plane to Glasgow
- (book/reserve) bus (tickets) to airport
- (sort out their) accommodation/youth hostel/somewhere to stay (in Scotland)/place to stay

4. • plane/flight delayed one hour/had to wait an hour for plane to leave
  plane/flight delayed because of fog/(bad) mist/weather
- one friend/one of the group lost (his) wallet/purse

5. • their room/the room for 5/the room they had booked not available/not free/double-booked
  or
- they had to find another (youth-)hostel

6. *Any two from:*
- big/large billiards/snooker/pool room/hall
- <u>lots of/many/full of</u> games and books
- barbecue/BBQ in garden
  or
- small garden

7. • so many shops
  or
- lot(s) of/many shops in town/city centre

8. • looked at/around/visited/went to see the castle
  or
- strolled/wandered/meandered along Princes Street
  walked along/up/down Princes Street

9. *Any two from:*
- rich/strong/wonderful/great culture
  a place of culture/very cultural/lots of culture
- exciting/good/wicked/buzzing/healthy night-life
- (very/really) good shopping/shops/shopping possibilities/shopping facilities
  lots of good shops
- wonderful/beautiful/spectacular/great countryside/nature/scenery/landscape
- lakes/lochs/Highlands worth seeing

10. • went to Inverness (when she was) in Year 7
    • school/student exchange
      one year Scots go to Hamburg and the next year
      Germans go to Inverness

11. *Any one from:*
    • get to know/meet new people
    • get to know/meet/discover/experience/learn
      about/see
      a different/an exciting/another culture/way of life
    • it was great/really good/lots of fun

SECTION B

Please see the table on pages 12–13 which provides details
of the criteria required to produce a good essay answer.

HIGHER GERMAN
READING AND DIRECTED WRITING
2009

SECTION I – READING

1. (a) *Any one of:*
   - what people/they enjoy about/in the summer (time)
   - people/they love/enjoy/everyone loves the sun, warmth/warm weather/heat and free time in the summer
   - sun, warmth and free time are the best things/their favourite things about summer

   (b) • how people use/spend free/leisure/spare time
   how one uses one's free time
   the use of free time
   what they do/did in their free time

2. (a) • they <u>had to/would/used to</u> walk/run, as there were no buses

   (b) • met/collected/picked up/fetched/got tourists from the ferry
   went to tourists at the ferry
   • took/carried/brought/dropped off/put their (suit)cases/ luggage/bags to guest houses/B&B/inn/hotel/place they were staying
   brought their cases to the guest house

   (c) *Any two from:*
   - worked in a milk(-shake) bar/milk-shake shop
   - went walking/hiking <u>a lot</u>/on <u>a lot of</u>/<u>many</u> walks <u>lots of</u> walking tours
   - <u>sometimes</u> went to the Baltic (on holiday).

3. • They took/brought food with them/they took their own food/they had their own food/lunch.
   • If/when they had the money, they bought/would buy <u>a bottle of</u> lemonade/(fizzy-)juice.

4. (a) *Any one of:*
   - They made/sewed/stitched/cut/tailored their own clothes/things.
     Clothes that they altered themselves.
   - Dresses and skirts/a dress and skirt
   - They rolled/bunched/pulled up/folded over/adjusted their skirts to turn them into mini-skirts.
     They wore skirts high as mini-skirts.

   (b) • (They wore) mini-skirts and shorts.
   OR
   • The summer colour was blue.

   (c) *Any one of:*
   - lots of/many colours are fashionable/topical/up-to-date/in fashion/in.
     the current trend is to wear lots of colours.
   - people often wear stripes/stripes are popular/worn a lot/often.
   - lots of colours and stripes.

5. (a) • The only parties were family ones/celebrations.
   Parties were a family thing.
   Parties would be for families.
   There were only family parties.
   They were only at family festivals.
   • The children/young people/you <u>had to</u> be home/in/in the house at/by midnight.
   You <u>had to</u> go back to the house/home by/for midnight.

   (b) • they go to the disco/clubbing/night-clubs <u>every weekend/most weekends/every week/at the weekends</u>.
   • go to/visit town/city festivals/parties/celebrations/fairs/fêtes/galas/fiestas.

6. • Oma Ingrid – sang hiking/hiker/rambling/walking songs/ they sang songs while they were walking/hiking.
   • Katrin Bredner – they recorded/taped their own voices/ music/tunes (on a cassette recorder) <u>and</u> listened to it.

7. • The sun was very/really important <u>to/for her</u>.
   She found the sun very important.
   • She/you/one <u>could/was able to/got to</u> relax/take it easy/unwind.

8. Wir sind aber nie in den Urlaub gefahren
   But/However/we never/did not ever go/went (away/anywhere)/would never go (away/anywhere)/never used to go (away/anywhere)/on holiday/vacation/for a holiday

   weil wir nicht genug Geld hatten
   because/as/since/we did not have/didn't have/hadn't enough money.

   Meine Mutter sagte oft zu uns Kinder:
   My mother/mum often said/used to say/would say to us children/kids

   ,,Ich möchte so gerne einmal mit euch in die Bergen fahren…"
   I would/I'd so/really like/I would/I'd so love to go/to travel/to drive/to the mountains with you/one day/some day/sometime/(just) once/.

   Sie wollte uns immer die Alpen zeigen.
   She always wanted/was wanting to show us the Alps.

SECTION II – DIRECTED WRITING

Category	Mark	Content	Accuracy	Language Resource – Variety, Range, Structures
Very Good	15	• All bullet points are covered fully, in a balanced way, including a number of complex sentences. • Some candidates may also provide additional information. • A wide range of verbs/verb forms, tenses and constructions is used. • Overall this comes over as a competent, well thought-out account of the event which reads naturally.	• The candidate handles all aspects of grammar and spelling accurately, although the language may contain some minor errors or even one more serious error. • Where the candidate attempts to use language more appropriate to post-Higher, a slightly higher number of inaccuracies need not detract from the overall very good impression.	• The candidate is comfortable with almost all the grammar used and generally uses a different verb or verb form in each sentence. • There is good use of a variety of tenses, adjectives, adverbs and prepositional phrases and, where appropriate, word order. • The candidate uses co-ordinating conjunctions and subordinate clauses throughout the writing. • The language flows well.
Good	12	• All bullet points are addressed, generally quite fully, and some complex sentences may be included. • The response to one bullet point may be thin, although other bullet points are dealt with in some detail. • The candidate uses a reasonable range of verbs/verb forms and other constructions.	• The candidate generally handles verbs and other parts of speech accurately but simply. • There may be some errors in spelling, adjective endings and, where relevant, case endings. • Use of accents may be less secure. • Where the candidate is attempting to use more complex vocabulary and structures, these may be less successful, although basic structures are used accurately. • There may be minor misuse of dictionary.	• There may be less variety in the verbs used. • The candidate is able to use a significant amount of complex sentences. • In one bullet point the language may be more basic than might otherwise be expected at this level. • Overall the writing will be competent, mainly correct, but pedestrian.
Satisfactory	9	• The candidate uses mainly simple, more basic sentences. • The language is perhaps repetitive and uses a limited range of verbs and fixed phrases not appropriate to this level. • In some examples, one or two bullet points may be less fully addressed. • In some cases, the content may be similar to that of good or very good examples, but with some serious accuracy issues.	• The verbs are generally correct, but basic. • Tenses may be inconsistent, with present tenses being used at times instead of past tenses. • There are quite a few errors in other parts of speech – personal pronouns, gender of nouns, adjective endings, cases, singular/plural confusion – and in the use of accents. • Some prepositions may be inaccurate or omitted eg I went the town. • While the language may be reasonably accurate in three or four bullet points, in the remaining two control of the language structure may deteriorate significantly. • Overall, there is more correct than incorrect.	• The candidate copes with the past tense of some verbs. • A limited range of verbs is used to address some of the bullet points. • Candidate relies on a limited range of vocabulary and structures. • Occasionally, the past participle is incorrect or the auxiliary verb is omitted. • Sentences may be basic and mainly brief. • There is minimal use of adjectives, probably mainly after "is" eg The boss was helpful. • The candidate has a weak knowledge of plurals. • There may be several spelling errors eg reversal of vowel combinations.

Category	Mark	Content	Accuracy	Language Resource – Variety, Range, Structures
Unsatisfactory	6	• In some cases the content may be basic. • In other cases there may be little difference in content between Satisfactory and Unsatisfactory. • The language is repetitive, with undue reliance on fixed phrases and a limited range of common basic verbs such as *to be, to have, to play, to watch.* • While the language used to address the more predictable bullet points may be accurate, serious errors occur when the candidate attempts to address the less predictable areas. • The Directed Writing may be presented as a single paragraph.	• Ability to form tenses is inconsistent. • In the use of the perfect tense the auxiliary verb is omitted on a number of occasions. • There may be confusion between the singular and plural form of verbs. • There are errors in many other parts of speech – gender of nouns, cases, singular/plural confusion, spelling and, where appropriate, word order. • Several errors are serious, perhaps showing mother tongue interference. • There may be one sentence which is not intelligible to a sympathetic native speaker. • One area may be very weak. • Overall, there is more incorrect than correct.	• The candidate copes mainly only with the predictable language required at the earlier bullet points. • The verbs "was" and "went" may also be used correctly. • There is inconsistency in the use of various expressions, especially verbs. • Sentences are more basic. • An English word may appear in the writing or a word may be omitted. • There may be an example of serious dictionary misuse.
Poor	3	• The content and language may be very basic. • However, in many cases the content may be little different from that expected at Unsatisfactory or even at Satisfactory.	• Many of the verbs are incorrect or even omitted. • There are many errors in other parts of speech – personal pronouns, gender of nouns, adjective endings, cases, singular/plural confusion, word order, spelling. • Prepositions are not used correctly. • The language is probably inaccurate throughout the writing. • Some sentences may not be understood by a sympathetic native speaker.	• The candidate cannot cope with more than 1 or 2 basic verbs, frequently *had* and *was*. • The candidate displays almost no knowledge of past tenses of verbs. • Verbs used more than once may be written differently on each occasion. • The candidate has a very limited vocabulary. • Several English or "made-up" words may appear in the writing. • There are examples of serious dictionary misuse.
Very Poor	0	• The content is very basic OR • The candidate has not completed at least three of the core bullet points.	• (Virtually) nothing is correct. • Most of the errors are serious. • Very little is intelligible to a sympathetic native speaker.	• The candidate copes only with "have" and "am". • Very few words are correctly written in the foreign language. • English words are used. • There may be several examples of mother tongue interference. • There may be several examples of serious dictionary misuse.

HIGHER GERMAN LISTENING/WRITING 2009

SECTION A

1. 4,500

2. (a) • relatively few(er)/only a few/very few/not many/not a lot/too little/very little/hardly any/not very many/not enough for the number of people fewer/less places than the number of students.

(b) *Any one from:*
   • to leave/move out of Görlitz/their town/home/ parents/friends.
   • to go to/find/get a place/one in another town/city/ place.
   • to move away/to another town.

3. *Any two from:*
   • not (so) easy.
   • missed her friends/family/home area.
   • knew nobody/did not know anyone.

4. • can bring/take friends home at any time/no matter how late it is/until as late as she wants/when(ever) she wants/at any time of the day/regardless of the time/as late as she likes.
   • at weekend can sleep (in)/lie in/stay in bed as late/long as you want/long lies.
   can get up whenever he wants.
   sleep all weekend.

5. *Any three from:*
   • You have to/must/having to do everything (for) yourself
   She has to/must/having to do everything (for) herself.
   • (You have/she has to do) your/her own shopping/the shopping/buy things for herself/buy everything/shop for herself/pay for her own shopping.
   • (You have) to clean yourself/(she has) to clean herself/do your/her own cleaning/the cleaning/the housework/clean the house.
   • (You have/she has) to budget/make sure money lasts to the end of the month/work out the finances/divide up the money (for the month)/manage your money/keep track of your money/organise your finances for each month.

6. • She is earning/making/earns/gets/makes more money (than friends in Görlitz).
   She has been able to earn more money than her friends.
   She is better paid in Hamburg.
   (You get/earn/make) more money.
   Her old friends in Görlitz earn less than her.

7. (a) • A colleague/employee/trainee/someone took/was ill.

(b) • She wanted to live/stay in North(ern) Germany.

8. • They went/travelled/came with her to Hamburg.
   They went to Hamburg together.
   They took her to Hamburg.
   • They looked/searched together/with her for a flat/house/ somewhere to stay/a place to stay/live/accommodation.
   They helped her look for/find/get/visit a flat.
   They viewed flats with her.
   They found a flat with her.
   • They bought her/paid for everything/things/stuff/items/what she needed/everything she needed for the flat/house.
   They helped her buy everything for the flat.

9. • Hamburg is (very/so) much/a lot/lots bigger/larger.
   One is a big city; the other is a town.
   • The people speak/have/talk a different/their own dialect.
   The dialect is different/there are different dialects.
   The people speak a different kind of German.

10. *Any one from:*
   • To see/meet (up with)/visit/catch up with her old/childhood friends.
   To see the friends she had there.
   To see her friends again.

11. • She is more independent/grown-up/self-sufficient/self-reliant/mature.
   She is more of an adult.
   She has gained in independence.
   She can now stand on her own two feet.

SECTION B

Category	Mark	Content	Accuracy	Language Resource – Variety, Range, Structures
Very Good	10	• The topic is covered fully, in a balanced way, including a number of complex sentences. • Some candidates may also provide additional information. • A wide range of verbs/verb forms and constructions is used. There may also be a variety of tenses. • Overall this comes over as a competent, well thought-out response to the task which reads naturally.	• The candidate handles all aspects of grammar and spelling accurately, although the language may contain some minor errors or even one more serious error. • Where the candidate attempts to use language more appropriate to post-Higher, a slightly higher number of inaccuracies need not detract from the overall very good impression.	• The candidate is comfortable with almost all the grammar used and generally uses a different verb or verb form in each sentence. • There is good use of a variety of tenses, adjectives, adverbs and prepositional phrases and, where appropriate, word order. • The candidate uses co-ordinating conjunctions and subordinate clauses throughout the writing. • The language flows well.
Good	8	• The topic is addressed, generally quite fully, and some complex sentences may be included. • The candidate uses a reasonable range of verbs/verb forms and other constructions.	• The candidate generally handles verbs and other parts of speech accurately but simply. • There may be some errors in spelling, adjective endings and, where relevant, case endings. • Use of accents may be less secure. • Where the candidate is attempting to use more complex vocabulary and structures, these may be less successful, although basic structures are used accurately. • There may be minor misuse of dictionary.	• There may be less variety in the verbs used. • Most of the complex sentences use co-ordinating conjunctions, and there may also be examples of subordinating conjunctions where appropriate. • At times the language may be more basic than might otherwise be expected at this level. • Overall the writing will be competent, mainly correct, but pedestrian.
Satisfactory	6	• The candidate uses mainly simple, more basic sentences. • The language is perhaps repetitive and uses a limited range of verbs and fixed phrases not appropriate to this level. • The topic may not be fully addressed. • In some cases, the content may be similar to that of good or very good examples, but with some serious accuracy issues.	• The verbs are generally correct, but basic. • Tenses may be inconsistent. • There are quite a few errors in other parts of speech – personal pronouns, gender of nouns, adjective endings, cases, singular/plural confusion – and in the use of accents. • Some prepositions may be inaccurate or omitted eg I go the town. • While the language may be reasonably accurate at times, the language structure may deteriorate significantly in places. • Overall, there is more correct than incorrect and there is the impression overall that the candidate can handle tenses.	• The candidate copes with the present tense of most verbs. • A limited range of verbs is used. • Candidate relies on a limited range of vocabulary and structures. • Where the candidate attempts constructions with modal verbs, these are not always successful. • Sentences may be basic and mainly brief. • There is minimal use of adjectives, probably mainly after "is" eg My friend is reliable. • The candidate has a weak knowledge of plurals. • There may be several spelling errors eg reversal of vowel combinations.

Category	Mark	Content	Accuracy	Language Resource – Variety, Range, Structures
Unsatisfactory	4	• In some cases the content may be basic. • In other cases there may be little difference in content between Satisfactory and Unsatisfactory. • The language is repetitive, with undue reliance on fixed phrases and a limited range of common basic verbs such as *to be, to have, to play, to watch*. • While the language used to address the more predictable aspects of the task may be accurate, serious errors occur when the candidate attempts to address a less predictable aspect. • The Personal Response may be presented as a single paragraph.	• Ability to form tenses is inconsistent. • In the use of the perfect tense the auxiliary verb is omitted on a number of occasions. • There may be confusion between the singular and plural form of verbs. • There are errors in many other parts of speech – gender of nouns, cases, singular/plural confusion – and in spelling and, where appropriate, word order. • Several errors are serious, perhaps showing mother tongue interference. • There may be one sentence which is not intelligible to a sympathetic native speaker. • Overall, there is more incorrect than correct.	• The candidate copes mainly only with predictable language. • There is inconsistency in the use of various expressions, especially verbs. • Sentences are more basic. • An English word may appear in the writing or a word may be omitted. • There may be an example of serious dictionary misuse.
Poor	2	• The content and language may be very basic. • However, in many cases the content may be little different from that expected at Unsatisfactory or even at Satisfactory.	• Many of the verbs are incorrect or even omitted. • There are many errors in other parts of speech – personal pronouns, gender of nouns, adjective endings, cases, singular/plural confusion – and in spelling and word order. • Prepositions are not used correctly. • The language is probably inaccurate throughout the writing. • Some sentences may not be understood by a sympathetic native speaker.	• The candidate cannot cope with more than 1 or 2 basic verbs, frequently "has" and "is". • Verbs used more than once may be written differently on each occasion. • The candidate has a very limited vocabulary. • Several English or "made-up" words may appear in the writing. • There are examples of serious dictionary misuse.
Very Poor	0	• The content is very basic	• (Virtually) nothing is correct. • Most of the errors are serious. • Very little is intelligible to a sympathetic native speaker.	• The candidate copes only with "have" and "am". • Very few words are correctly written in the foreign language. • English words are used. • There may be several examples of mother tongue interference. • There may be several examples of serious dictionary misuse

Hey! I've done it

Published by Bright Red Publishing Ltd, 6 Stafford Street, Edinburgh, EH3 7AU
Tel: 0131 220 5804, Fax: 0131 220 6710, enquiries: sales@brightredpublishing.co.uk,
www.brightredpublishing.co.uk

Official SQA answers to 978-1-84948-060-4
2006-2009